Arizona

Quartzsite Area

Volume 3

UNEXPECTED BEAUTY

"Everything He has made pretty in its time."
Ecclesiastes 3:11

A picture Book of things you might see around Quartzsite.
Or, should I say **things you may have MISSED.**

The beauty of spring and early summer

As seen thru the eyes and camera of Joe Lange and Tootie Jacobs

©Joe Lange, D.J.Jacobs 2010

It is only 6:15 am and the place is already abuzz with activity. Only one day to gather the 'Manna' and these blossoms will close forever. However, there will be plenty of new ones tomorrow.

Arizona's State flower
Saguaro Blossom

The creamy, silk-like blossoms offer a friendly invitation to come and feast.

From the Gold Nugget Rd. overpass, east of Quartzsite.

Castle Dome

The Sonora Desert – The Lushest Desert on the Planet

Miss Arizona Desert

This Fishhook cactus only grows
about 8" tall and 3" wide.
It put on this gorgeous crown,
then did it again a few weeks later
only a row down.
I think it did it three times.

Spectacular it is –
but watch out for those hooks
they're very unforgiving…

The **Mourning Dove** (*Zenaida macroura*) is a member of the dove family (Columbidae). The bird is also called the **Western Turtle Dove** or the **American Mourning Dove** or **Rain Dove**, and formerly was known as the **Carolina Pigeon** or **Carolina Turtledove**. It is one of the most abundant and widespread of all North American birds. It is also the leading gamebird, with up to 70 million birds shot annually in the U.S., both for sport and for meat. Its ability to sustain such pressure stems from its prolific breeding: in warm areas, one pair may raise up to six broods a year. Its plaintive *woo-oo-oo-oo* call gives the bird its name. The wings can make an unusual whistling sound upon take-off and landing, and the bird is a strong flier, capable of speeds up to 88 km/h (55 mph).

The clutch size is almost always two eggs. Incubation takes two weeks. Fledging takes place in about 11–15 days.

Mourning Doves are prolific breeders. In warmer areas, these birds may raise up to six broods in a season.[11] This fast breeding is essential because mortality is high. Each year, mortality can reach 58% a year for adults and 69% for the young.[18]

From Wikipedia free encyclopedia

As these pictures show, doves will nest anywhere that they are able to put their eggs. Their nests are not anything like most birds build, but a few twigs on a limb, table, wall hanging, sill of an opened window, in my truck, in the tongue of a 5th wheel, or just about anywhere.

Doves make good pets. If you feed them they will soon come into your house to find out why you haven't put the food out yet.

I sat out each evening at the same time and place, and soon the doves were feeding at my feet, as well other birds including Quails. The Mourning Doves seem to be the tamest.

The large pinkish-tan ones are Ringnecks, the long-beaked ones with white strips along the side of the wings are Whitewings, and the tiny ones are Incas.

To many, these birds are a nuisance; nesting everywhere and messing on everything. If you don't want the nuisance don't feed them.

Tootie

These flowers are spectacular to look at up close, but they are more than that, they are lifeblood to the creatures that depend on them. These black and white bees are busy all day long in these flowers. In the top inset you can see him sipping nectar with his long tongue-like proboscis, sort of like a butterfly would do.

This Desert Iguana is about 16" long. Isn't he gorgeous?

A little Side Blotched Lizard

Hey, you kids get down; I don't have any more candy.

Modern Imitation Saguaros?

Somehow man's inventions are no match for our Creators'.

Take a closer look
at the flowers on
the facing page.

Marvelous indeed…

Traveling south on 95 towards Yuma, keep your eyes open for stunning sights like this. Ocotillo, Paloverde, Rabbit Brush and Creosote Bush make a nice combination to please the visual senses.

Bats are the primary pollinators of the Saguaro's night blooming flowers, that stay open into the next day, then bees and Doves seem to be the main pollinators. The flowers appear April through June and the sweet, ruby-colored fruit matures by late June. These photos were taken 5-30-10, in the afternoon. Here the flowers are closing. We should have come earlier in the day for blossom photos. Didn't know.

Hedgehog

There it is… a tiny and inconspicuous little plant growing in the wash. But take a closer look… such beauty, gone unnoticed by most.

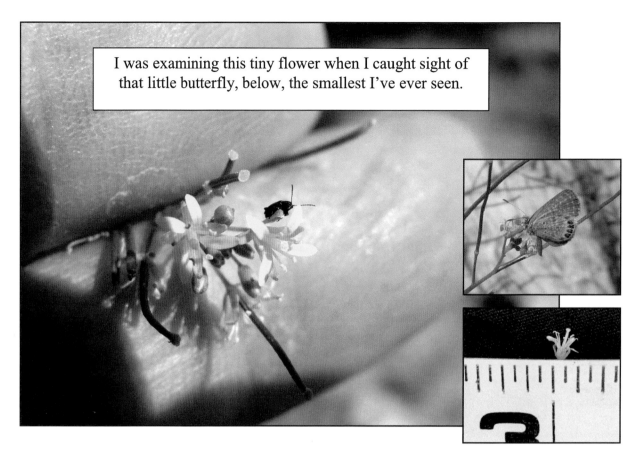

I was examining this tiny flower when I caught sight of that little butterfly, below, the smallest I've ever seen.

Take the time to stop and look – you'll be amazed by Unexpected Beauty.

I figured her at about ¾ inch wide.

Depositing the next generation.

Does this stir your imagination? Who or what is that in the lower left???

This is most unusual. I have seen this pattern a couple times looking ENE from town. ???

The Red Racer is the most often seen snake in the desert. They are the fastest too, racing along with their heads up, like cobras, at up to 7mph. Be aware... they have a mean disposition and will bite. Although not venomous their bite can tear your skin and be painful. It is best to just look; then leave them alone to eat mice, lizards, small snakes and birds.

Palm Canyon straight ahead

Soaking up the last rays of the day, this little guy is curled up in a hole in the side of the rock facing west, as the sun is setting. He is actually nearly perpendicular to the ground, but he's hanging in there.

Bunkers like this were used to safely store explosives.

Little Brown Myotis

Myotis lucifugus

As suggested by the bat's name, its fur is uniformly dark brown and glossy on the back and upper parts with slightly paler, greyish fur underneath. Wing membranes are dark brown on a typical wingspan of 22–27 cm (8.7–11 in).[2] Ears are small and black with a short, rounded tragus. Adult bats are typically 6–10 cm (2.4–3.9 in) long and weigh 5–14 grams (0.2–0.5 oz). All teeth including molars are relatively sharp, as is typical for an insectivore, and canines are prominent to enable grasping hard-bodied insects in flight.

Little brown bats are insectivores, eating moths, wasps, beetles, gnats, mosquitoes, midges and mayflies, among others. Since many of their preferred meals are insects with an aquatic life stage, such as mosquitoes, they prefer to roost near water. They echolocate to find their prey. Often they will catch larger prey with a wingtip, transfer it to a cup formed by their tail, then eat it - smaller prey are usually just caught in the mouth. They often use the same routes over and over again every night, flying 3-6 meters high above water or among trees. An adult can sometimes fill its stomach in 15 minutes; young have more difficulty. If they do not catch any food, they will enter a torpor similar to hibernation that day, awakening at night to hunt again.   **From Wikipedia, the free encyclopedia**

I was at the Quartzsite Laundromat one day when one of the employees mentioned that there was a bat on the concrete under a table out the back door. In volume 1 we showed a bat we rescued from a parking lot. So I went out to see it. Wow, so small. OK, another rescue… So the employee gave me a small soup cup to put it in.

I recalled that the Game and Fish Dept. had told me that a bat could not take off from the ground and needed to be put in a tree or on a wall so it could fly off when it got dark.

So Tootie and I felt confident that if we slipped it out of the soup cup onto my kitchen table, I would be able to take some close-up pictures. So we opened the cup and slid the little feller onto the table where, to our great surprise, in an instant, he made a quick dash off the table and was now flying back and forth thru my motor home. All he wanted was to find a place where he could finish his nap.

After a few pictures, he was sent off into the dark to get back to work eating bugs.

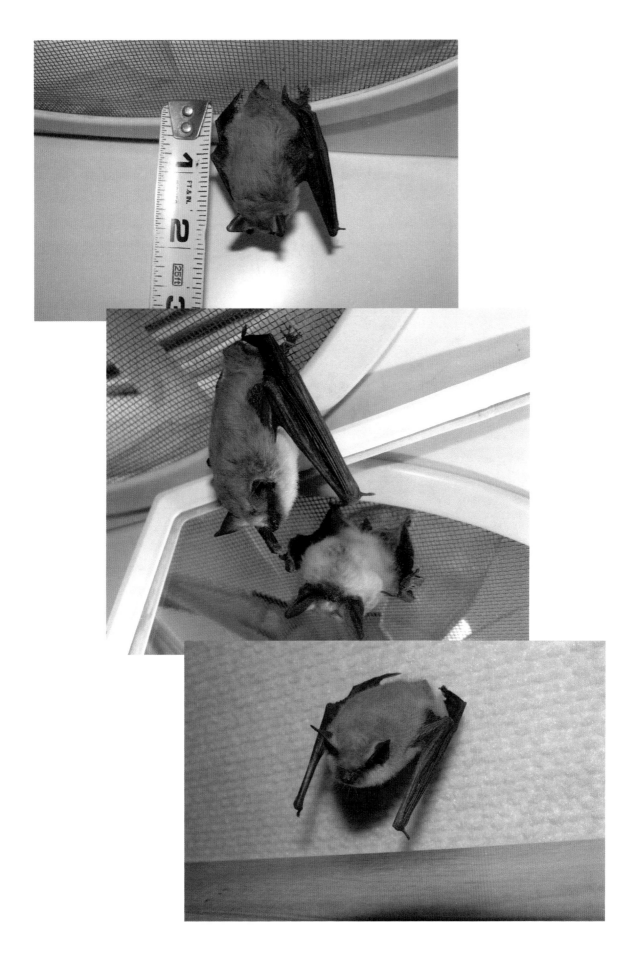

The Ironwood blossoms (left) are nearly invisible, and the leaves are gone.

But when caught in the beams of the setting sun, they show up beautifully.

Pencil cactus. You wouldn't even notice these driving by.
Blossoms are only about 1" in diameter and the color is subtle.

     Larrea tridentata, known as **creosote bush** (or **chaparral** when used as a medicinal herb) and "Gobernadora" in Mexico (Spanish for "Governess", because of its ability to inhibit the growing of other plants around and gain more water), is a flowering plant in the family Zygophyllaceae. It is a prominent species in the Mojave, Sonoran, and Chihuahuan Deserts of western North America, including portions of California, Arizona, Nevada, Utah, New Mexico and western Texas in the United States, and northern Chihuahua in Mexico.

     The whole plant exhibits a characteristic odor of creosote, from which the common name derives.

     They have peculiar regularity in the spacing of individual plants within a stand. Creosote bush stands tend to resemble man-made orchards in the even placement of plants. Originally, it was assumed that the plant produced some sort of water-soluble inhibitor that prevented the growth of other bushes near mature, healthy bushes. Now, however, it has been shown that the root systems of mature creosote plants are simply so efficient at absorbing water that fallen seeds nearby cannot accumulate enough water to germinate, effectively creating dead zones around every plant. It also seems that all plants within a stand grow at approximately the same rate, and that the creosote bush is a very long-living plant.

From Wikipedia, the free encyclopedia

Now THAT'S what I'm talkin' about!
Who would have EXPECTED to see such beauty?
NO! I MEAN THE FLOWER.
A little yellow bouquet lined with snow white pedals.

Like tiny fiber-optic strands glowing in the sun,
these little fibers will carry their elongated seeds
to a fertile new location and start a new plant.
AND LIFE GOES ON.

Many individual parts make up this beautiful thistle flower.

This tiny Desert Lily plant only gets about 8" tall.

This was the only flower in sight. It was on a vine coursing thru the cactus. It was truly unexpected to see such beauty in such a small and inconspicuous flower. Look at the perfect detail.

I was driving back to Quartzsite when I noticed this bluish bush alongside the highway. I stopped, and to my great surprise, this is what I found.
This is what I'm talking about when I say "UNEXPECTED Beauty".

Indigo Bush

Scorpion Weed (That is not a scorpion on the leaf, but a tiny, tiny Crab Spider.)
There are about 130 species of crab spiders in North America.

Range Ratany – breathtaking tiny flowers, and look at that seed pod; notice the barbs on the ends – typical Arizona. The whole plant is full of spikes.

Curved-Billed Thrasher
Related to Mockingbirds, he's singing his beautiful song on and on and on.

House Finch

Teddy Bear (Jumping) Cholla

Looking out across the desert, these blooms are pretty inconspicuous. Tootie and I were very excited on catching sight of them. Then we saw them everywhere, but not for long; remember, each flower only lasts one day. We are sure glad we came out today, for this real 'unexpected' delight.

Buckhorn Cholla (or Staghorn, I can't tell them apart)

Grey Fox

In early April, while in the mountains east of Quartzsite, we were looking for old ruins of old stone buildings and old mines, we spotted a beautiful grey fox. It didn't seem to be trying to get away very fast as most fox do. We wondered what could be responsible for her lack of action. We tossed her some hot dogs which she tried to eat. We were able to get a lot of shots and it wasn't until we put the pictures on the computer that we could see that she had a lot of Cholla spines in her mouth, feet pads, and many other places, needless to say we felt very sad for her. It seems that the creatures that live in the desert have a real tough time!   Tootie

Palo Verde and Ironwood dress up the desert nicely.

Dome Rock – Quartzsite, AZ

These are the flowers you see on this and the facing page.

Pincushion Flower

Brittle Bush or Rabbit Brush

Desert Mallow

On the Colorado River south of Ehrenberg, with Blyhe in the far distance.

Ocotillo

Narrowleaf Climbing Milkweed

Desert Mistletoe, a mystery to Joe and I for some time. We talked about the big clumps of something that we did think was some kind of parasite and also that it seemed to kill the tree that it was on. What we did find is that it is a **"partial parasite"**, because it generates its own chlorophyll photosynthesis, but it also draws both water and nutrients from its host tree or shrub which it sometimes kills eventually. It is good for something though, the reddish berries are food for several kinds of birds and small animals. The flower is small and hard to see, the color being greenish. Male and female flowers are on different trees. The female flowers produce the pinkish berries seen below.

Blue Palo Verde

Yellow Palo Verde

Ironwood – Arizona's State Tree

At a distance just looking like a profusion of mauve and green, a closer look reveals a marvel of creation.

OK, OK, here we go with the toes again. Really I just did that to demonstrate the size if these tiny flowers, **really**. You wouldn't even look for a flower in that dried up plant. What was it like in full bloom?

Gambles
Quail

Female Quail

Flycatcher

Huh ?

Oriole

Desert Mallow

I've got only five words for this,

Mm, mm, mm, mm, mmmm!

Now this is beauty only a mother could love…

The Sonora Desert is home to many species of wildlife, large and small.

Along the Hwy 95 corridor
Who'da thunk it???

Fairy Duster

Red Racer

When the snakes see me coming they run and hide in a hole.
Then when;

> They were looking out to see
> If I was looking back to see
> If they were looking out at me

I'd take their picture.

Both good snakes
to have around
your place.

But should be left
alone; they both
have grouchy
dispositions.

Gopher Snake

It's near the end of June and everything is pretty dried up. But on the way from Quartzsite to Blythe this silvery bush, slightly lavender, caught my eye. I don't know what it is but found it unusually beautiful in its own way.

We come across these breathtaking beauties out at Rainbow Acres. Argentine
Giants they are called. The flowers can be 8 or 9" wide. It seems a shame that they
only last one day each. I don't know what the lower right one is, but look at the
buds. Thanks to you folks at Rainbow Acres, you have some spectacular gardens.

Saguaro seeds often take root in the shade of a host plant.
Then they outlive their host to go on to live up to 150 yrs.
It takes about 75 years to develop arms. Here the host is
an Ironwood tree. (Creosote or Chaparral in the foreground)

Rick says:

"My love of the State of Arizona began when I visited my Mom and Step Dad in the Mesa area one winter in the early 90's. At the time I was living in the Canadian Arctic, so traveling to sunny and warm Arizona was a dream. Just before I retired, my wife Debbie and I took all our vacation days and spent 2 months with friends camped on the BLM land south of Quartzsite. We have continued to spend most of the winters at Quartzsite since then. With so much to do around Quartzsite and since its close enough to take day trips to Mexico, Phoenix, Palm Springs and Vegas, we found it the perfect place to stay. I started prospecting for Gold after talking to others in the park and old timers around town. My search for the Mother Lode continues, but as long as I see colour in the Gold Pan, it's a good day. We plan on returning to Quartzsite from Canada for many years to come. We have met a lot of very nice people that have become very good friends."

These shots were taken in the mountains southwest of Quartzsite. In this area, everywhere you look, there are staked mining claims. We were looking for just that, MINES! We asked a few miners if we could take a few pictures and tried to tell them what we were doing. Most just sort of ignored us, but we did come across a very nice man by the name of Forrest. He took us down into his diggings explaining what each tool and tunnel was being used for. One tunnel is where they eat lunch out of the hot summer sun. Forrest said "I am not doing this to get rich; I do it because I enjoy it".

The nugget in the lower right picture is called a "picker" because you can 'pick' it out with your fingers.

Thanks Forrest…

Tootie

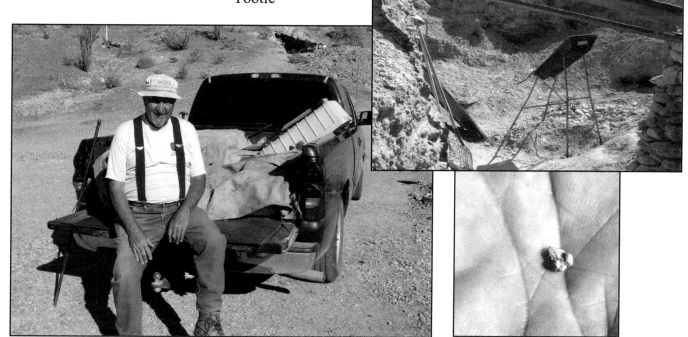

The cabin at the Apache Chief Mine. SE of Quartzsite, off of Gold Nugget Road.

"MOE
I am no Moe. May I rest in peace. Jan 2003"